Hunting and Herding Dogs

Dog Tales:
True Stories About Amazing Dogs

Dog Tales:
True Stories About Amazing Dogs

Hunting and Herding Dogs

Marie-Therese Miller

CHELSEA CLUBHOUSE

An Imprint of Chelsea House Publishers

Hunting and Herding Dogs

© 2007 by Infobase Publishing

Chelsea Clubhouse
An imprint of Infobase Publishing
132 West 31st Street
New York NY 10001

ISBN-10: 0-7910-9038-8
ISBN-13: 978-0-7910-9038-1

Library of Congress Cataloging-in-Publication Data
Miller, Marie-Therese.
    Hunting and herding dogs / Marie-Therese Miller.
        p. cm. — (Dog tales, true stories about amazing dogs)
    Includes bibliographical references and index.
    ISBN 0-7910-9038-8 (hardcover)
    1. Hunting dogs—Juvenile literature.   2. Herding dogs—Juvenile literature. I. Title. II. Series.
SF428.5.M55 2007
636.75—dc22

Development Editor: Anna Prokos
Text Design: Annie O'Donnell
Cover Design: Ben Peterson

Printed in the United States of America

Bang FOF 10 9 8 7 6 5 4 3 2 1

This book is printed on acid-free paper.

Contents

Chasing Down the Fox

Just after dawn, a pack of foxhounds races up a hill. They swiftly dash across a flowing stream, in hot pursuit of a bushy-tailed red fox. Behind the pack, riders on horses follow the hounds, hoping to catch a glimpse of the **quarry**. The fox leads the hounds and riders on a multiple-mile chase before it disappears into the safety of its hole. For now, the hunt is over and the dogs reluctantly take a break.

Foxhunt scenes like this have been part of the United States's history since colonial times. Even President

Foxhounds get ready for an exciting foxhunt as they listen for directions from the huntsman.

George Washington—along with his hounds—took part in foxhunts at his home in Mount Vernon, Virginia. Back then, though, the object of a foxhunt was to kill a fox. Farmers viewed the foxes as pests that attacked sheep and chickens. Luckily, times have changed for foxes. In modern foxhunts, no fox is supposed to be killed or hurt. Today's foxhunts are for sport or hobby, both for the people and for the dogs involved.

THE ROMBOUT HUNT DOGS

The 50 American foxhounds that live at the Rombout Hunt in Clinton, New York, are descendants of the

WHO'S ON THE CREW

With hounds hot on the trail of a fox, it's easy for the dogs to run too quickly or even to stray from the pack. That's where various members of the hunt staff can help. Foxhunt staff members make sure to keep the hunt—and the dogs—moving safely and smoothly.

Because a foxhunt can continue for miles, the master of the foxhunt makes sure that the group can move across private property. If a disagreement occurs between property owners and the group, the master tries to solve it peacefully.

By pointing a whip and giving commands, a **whipper-in** directs the hounds during a foxhunt. This professional keeps the pack together, and he's always on the lookout for hounds that go too fast or too slow. "Get on!" he'll command to a slowpoke hound that needs to hurry along. If the pack is moving too far ahead, the whipper-in will slow the group down. They cannot be allowed to catch the fox.

A whipper-in is also responsible for the dogs' safety. If a car poses a danger to a hound, the whipper-in will shout "get over" to guide the animal to safety. The Rombout Hunt staff carries radios and warns handlers of dangerous conditions that might threaten the pack, such as heavy traffic, a change in weather, or out-of-the-ordinary terrain.

Participants who ride on horseback and follow the pack are called the field. The field master, who's in charge of the riders, makes sure the field rides behind the hounds at all times. If a rider moves in front of the pack, the fox might get frightened and turn toward the hounds. That could mean serious trouble for the fox. Field masters also make sure that the participants follow rules and speak softly. Loud noises or laughter could distract the hounds from their work. Everyone works together to ensure a fun and successful hunt.

On the day of a foxhunt, the hounds at Rombout Hunt eagerly wait to be released from their kennels.

hounds of early America. Like their ancestors, these dogs are trained specifically for foxhunting. They know exactly what to do when it's time to chase their quarry, whether it is a fox or a coyote.

On the day of a chase, a Rombout **huntsman** releases the foxhound pack from their kennels. The huntsman's job is to control and direct the hounds. He rides with the pack and gives them commands, both with his voice and with signals blown on a horn. At first, the huntsman allows the pack to spread out and search for the fox. When the hounds pick up the scent of fox, they make deep, melodic sounds. In foxhunting vocabulary, this is known as "giving tongue." If the hounds find a fox and start the chase, the huntsman will blow short bursts of several notes. This signal, called "gone away," lets the hounds and riders know the hunt has begun.

DRESSED TO IMPRESS

Like a karate kid who earns colored belts, the foxhunt participant can secure the honor of wearing the colors of his or her particular hunt club on the jacket collar. A person who distinguishes himself in the field and volunteers many hours to benefit the hunt club may be awarded his colors. He would also be permitted to attach brass buttons, which are adorned with the initials of the club, to his coat.

Those with their colors get the privilege of riding toward the front of the field. Members who have had their colors longer ride in front of club newcomers.

The participants in foxhunts are certainly chic dressers. During the formal Rombout Hunt season, the staff and the gentlemen of the field, who have earned their colors, wear traditional scarlet coats, white britches, and stock ties, a long piece of material that is wrapped around the neck. The women wear navy or black coats.

Hunting garb looks quite proper and fashionable, but foxhunt clothing is functional, too. The stock tie, for instance, can be used to bandage an injured hound, horse, or rider.

The foxhounds chase the quarry across vast meadows and over rock walls. If the huntsman needs to change directions, he might give one or two blasts on the horn to let the hounds know his new location. Close at the hounds' heels, the field follows. The horses and their riders sail over fences and trot around trees, keeping in step with the quick fox.

Hounds and the hunt participants have to be ready for just about anything during a foxhunt. No one can predict the way a foxhunt will go. Just ask Joy Imperati, the field master of the Rombout Hunt. She recalls one particular hunt when the hounds quickly caught the scent of a fox. What happened next was surprising: The fox crawled from its hole, raced to a nearby stream for a drink, and dove back into its home. "That must have been the shortest hunt in history," Imperati remembers.

The fox's actions aren't the only things that impact a foxhunt. The weather, wind, and temperature can affect the strength of the scent that the dogs must follow. On hot summer days, fresh dew on the grass keeps a fox scent strong for the dogs. They use their keen sense of smell and some vigorous training to **track** down the fox.

Raising Amazing Foxhounds

American foxhounds are skilled hunters. They're born with an acute sense of smell and a strong hunting instinct. For these reasons, foxhounds don't require much training. The Rombout Hunt, however, likes to take certain steps to ensure the hounds' hunting success.

Breeding time is the first step in forming a foxhound's skill. The Rombout staff takes time to select compatible male and female hounds for breeding. The dogs must be healthy and strong. Energetic

After puppies are born at Rombout Hunt, they live with their mother. A mother provides milk and warmth.

foxhounds can hunt for 20 to 30 miles (32 to 48 km) in a day. If the parent dogs can do this, chances are their pups will grow up healthy and energetic, too. The staff also chooses hounds that show strong hunt drives. They look for hounds that won't give up during a fox pursuit. Also, the quality of a hound's voice is an important factor. The hound must have a deep voice that can be heard over the hills and valleys of hunting terrain.

When the puppies are born, each dog receives a name that begins with the first letter of one of its parents' names. The trainers at Rombout Hunt select names that match the pup hound's personality.

STEPPING INTO TRAINING

The puppies need to learn lessons they can use during a foxhunt. At four months old, the pups are ready for their first days of training. They are taught to walk calmly on a leash without pulling or lagging behind their trainer. This time on the leash teaches the puppies to interact with humans, just as they will do during a hunt. At this time, the pups are also taught to respond when their names are being called, which will help during the hunt.

When the puppy is six months old, a length of chain is attached to its collar and then linked to the collar of a more experienced hound. With this couples collar, the puppy learns to walk properly in the pack. The collar is removed when the puppy isn't pulling its elder around or being pulled by its experienced mate.

Walking lessons like this are useful during a hunt, when the foxhound must be able to follow other dogs in its pack. It also teaches the puppies to interact with humans, just as they do during a hunt. During their walks, the puppies are taught to respond to their names being called. This skill comes in handy when the huntsman or whipper-in addresses the foxhound during a hunt.

Walking helps keep the puppies fit while increasing their stamina. Rombout Hunt's members take the foxhound pack for a 1 1/2-mile (2 km) walk each morning. As the group walks along the street, the puppies become accustomed to strangers and cars. The puppies also learn not to chase after the other dogs and cats they may meet during a hunt.

To step up the pack's stamina, the length and pace of the walks are increased gradually. During these longer jaunts, the hunt members ride horses so that

FOR SAFETY'S SAKE

The health and safety of the foxhounds are of key importance to the Rombout Hunt. Stephen Farrin, Rombout's former professional whipper-in, carefully keeps track of what the hounds eat. "The hounds are fed a high protein diet to keep them lean and fit," he says. To give their coats a healthy-looking shine, milk powder is added to their food. If these dogs were being raised in England, chances are they'd eat fresh meat. Some people believe feeding dogs meat increases their hunting drives.

Taking care of the hounds' living quarters is another important step to keep the hounds healthy. Rombout's whipper-in scrubs the dogs' kennels daily—even twice a day in warm weather. This extra work ensures that bacteria and viruses stay away so that the dogs aren't threatened by disease.

The foxhounds' safety is also a primary concern during the hunt. High-tech collars keep each dog in the pack from getting lost during a hunt. The tracking collars can send a signal to the staff to locate an animal that has strayed from the group.

the puppies become familiar with seeing and working with the horses.

By the time the puppies reach one year to 18 months old, they are ready to experience the hunt. Their first hunts occur in late summer, and trainers call these cub hunts. That's because both the young hounds and the fox cubs are learning the ways of the hunt. During the cubs' first few cub hunts, the huntsman pays close attention to the puppy pack. The huntsman teaches the puppies not to follow deer scent. Because deer run straight and fast, a deer chase could land the puppy stranded in the woods.

These early cub hunts give the young foxhounds a taste of the hunt excitement. The thrill encourages them to use their natural hunting ability to have successful foxhunts.

3

Dogs That Hunt

A hunter strides through the field. Close ahead, an English springer spaniel walks in a zigzag pattern. The dog is using his sense of smell to pick up the air scent of birds. All at once, the dog races straight toward a pheasant and flushes the bird into the air. The spaniel sits, so he will be safe while the hunter takes his shot. The bird falls and the dog is commanded to retrieve it. The pheasant will make an elegant supper for the hunter and his family.

A hunter walks through a field with his spaniel hunting dog by his side.

Dogs that hunt are placed in categories according to the job they perform during a hunt. The English springer spaniel and the cocker spaniel, for example, are types of flushing dogs. These dogs force **game birds**, such as pheasants, into the air from the brush. At that point, the hunter can take a clear shot, thanks to his hard-working dog that knows exactly what to do when it spots a game bird: **Flush** him out.

In addition to being top-notch flushing dogs, retrievers play a major role during a hunt. As their name suggests, retrievers pick up game that has been

English springer spaniels are good flushing dogs that force game birds into the air so the hunter can take a shot.

shot and carry it back to their owners. Labrador retrievers, golden retrievers, and Chesapeake Bay retrievers are often used for waterfowl hunting, such as during a duck hunt. Retrievers like to swim, so hunting water birds makes this a perfect job for this type of dog.

Labrador retrievers, for example, are physically designed for water work. They were originally bred on the island of Newfoundland and were used to help fisherman haul fish-filled nets from the water. These muscular dogs are powerful swimmers—and they're built for the water. A Labrador has a double coat of fur that keeps the dog warm when it has to go into icy ponds or cold rivers. The dog's coat is also water-repellent.

MANY SPECIALIZED HUNTING DOGS

Pointing dogs are normally used to hunt upland game birds, such as quail. English pointers and German shorthaired pointers are examples of point- ing dogs. These dogs use their pointing instinct to show the presence of prey. A pointer uses its nose to sniff through the air and locate an upland game bird. When the dog is close to the bird, it stops and points its front paw. The pointer's body and tail stiffen, its muzzle points toward the bird, and its paw stays lifted until its owner or hunting group flushes the bird.

The dog's point allows a hunter the chance to flush the bird when he is prepared to shoot. The pointer will stay still until the hunter arrives, careful not to disturb the bird. For this reason, pointer dogs can work farther away from a hunter than a flushing dog can. Sometimes, two or more handlers with pointing dogs spend the day hunting together. If one of the dogs points to a game bird, the other honors the point by taking a pointing stance a few steps back from

A pointer dog uses its instincts to locate a game bird and then stiffens its tail and body and points with its paw.

the first dog. You can imagine how impressive this would be when a hunting party has multiple pointing dogs, all honoring a point.

A hunter must carefully consider what specialty he wants his hunting dog to have. Once the hunter has decided what breed is best for his needs, he will have to spend months training the dog. Only then will the

SEARCHING FOR SLAVES

Today's hunting dogs are often trained to hunt for animals, and usually for the positive purpose of putting food on the family table. But in the 1800s, many hunting dogs were taught to track slaves who tried to escape to freedom. Bloodhounds, foxhounds, curs, and mixed-breed dogs were often used to find slaves.

Frederick Law Olmsted was a famous architect who founded the American landscape architecture. In addition to designing famous places, such as Central Park in New York City, Olmsted traveled around the American colonies during the Civil War era. He wrote about slavery and the terrible living conditions of slaves. Olmsted reported on the use of dogs to track slaves who had tried to run away. He explained how the dogs were trained to do this sad job. As a puppy, each canine was taught to sniff an article that belonged to a slave, such as a shirt or a sock. Then, that slave laid a scent trail for the dog to follow by running across fields and through the woods. The dog was rewarded with meat when he located the slave. This training readied the dogs for tracking slaves who tried to escape to freedom. When a dog hunted a runaway slave, he attempted to chase the slave up a tree, and not purposely hurt him or her.

Hunters who look for rabbits or badgers can enlist the help of terriers. These canines hunt animals that build underground burrows.

hunter and his dog be able to enjoy fruitful days of hunting together.

For people who hunt furred **game**, such as fox or raccoon, hounds are good dog choices. Hounds, such as the American foxhound, bloodhound, beagle, or basset hound, use their fine sense of smell to follow scents on the ground. They usually hunt with their noses pointing down, trying to sniff out the trail of furred animals. The hound lets the hunter know that he has found a scent track by vocalizing, or giving tongue.

Hunters who look for rabbits or badgers might turn to terrier dogs for help. The word *terrier* comes from the Latin word *terra*, which means "earth." Terriers, such as Cairn terriers, Jack Russell terriers, or Norwich terriers, are hunting dogs that "go to ground." They enter the holes that are homes to their prey. The dogs are used to hunt animals that may have **burrows** underground. Terriers might kill the game in its hole or chase it from its shelter to allow the hunter to take a shot.

Training for the Hunt

Raymond Cacchio is an expert hunting dog trainer who specializes in training dogs that hunt upland game birds, such as quail or pheasant. He works with a variety of dogs, including English springer spaniels, Labrador retrievers, and even standard poodles. Because many people don't always have the luxury of owning more than one type of hunting dog, Cacchio teaches each dog to multitask. The dogs learn to both flush and retrieve game.

Before Cacchio's expert training can be utilized, the hunter must choose a puppy that shows promise as a hunting dog. Cacchio tells potential owners to choose canine parents that are known for their hunting abilities or are champions in hunting field trials. He also advises choosing a puppy the handler likes, as the dog and the hunter will be constant companions. Some dog trainers say hunters should stay away from choosing shy pups, but Cacchio disagrees. He believes that a shy puppy could blossom into a skilled hunting dog.

Cacchio likes to reward hunting dogs as they learn. He trains with a giant bag of dog cookies close at hand. When the pup is 8 weeks old, it starts obedience training with Cacchio. The dog first learns to

SPECIALIZED TRAINING

Trainers know how to train dogs based on what dogs of the same breed can do best and what they need the dogs to do. The hunter teaching the retriever to fetch waterfowl, for example, will add water training to the mix. He may place the puppy in shallow water of a comfortable temperature. As the puppy grows, the trainer brings the dog to deeper and colder water. This helps the dog become used to the idea of jumping into water to seize quarry.

Trainers that teach pointing dogs concentrate on the point. Some experts train the pup to point at a bird wing attached to a fishing pole. Cacchio trains his pointing dogs by releasing quail into a field. Upon the birds' release, the pointer pup is let go.

sit because it will need to sit on command so it can remain safe when the hunter shoots. Also for safety, the puppy is taught to heel to the left of the handler, or to the opposite side of his gun arm. In addition, the puppy learns to come, which will be necessary when it retrieves the game bird.

Silence is often required in the hunting field so that the birds are not frightened away. Cacchio uses a variety of spoken commands, hand signals, and whistles when teaching the dogs obedience.

PLAYING WITH THE PUPS

Dogs that train with Cacchio often go for car rides with him. This enables the dog to get comfortable with vehicle travel so that it won't have a hard time

The pup usually runs up to the birds too quickly, causing them to fly. Their wings will make lots of noise and startle the puppy. The pointing pup soon learns to approach the birds slowly and to pause. The pup's instinct to point and his experience with the quail combine to help him master the pointing skill.

Terriers can be taught to find prey in underground holes with a trainer's use of a manmade "earth." The earth contains a series of tunnels in which the dog can hunt. The tunnels are scented with the game's odor. The prey is found at the end of the scent trail, but a cage protects it, so the dog can't harm it. With consistent practice, and rewards for finding the prey, terriers soon learn to become skilled hunters.

By interacting with children, puppies learn to stay calm during noisy situations.

as it rides to the hunting grounds with its owner. He also walks the puppy around town and lets the canine play with children. "Kids are the best thing for a puppy," the trainer says. By interacting with children and adults, puppies can become familiar with people and noisy situations. While hunting, they will need to stay calm around loud gunshots and other hunters and their dogs.

Cacchio and the pup play many games of fetch with a tennis ball, which teaches the puppy that retrieving items can be loads of fun. When the pup is about

6 months old, Cacchio introduces the sound of shotgun fire into the game. As the dog enthusiastically chases the tennis ball, Cacchio shoots the weapon. The point of this exercise is to allow the dog to connect the loud noise with a good time. The dog must learn to take a shotgun blast in stride because a hunting dog that is afraid of gunfire is useless to a hunter.

Many hunting dogs have to learn to stay several yards away from their hunters. Cacchio has a way to teach the dogs to stay close ahead of their handler and not run after game birds that are too far away. He packs a game bag with dead pigeons and goes to a field with the pup. Next, he releases the dog and lets it run a certain distance. Then, he calls the dog back. When the dog arrives next to Cacchio, it sees a pigeon on the ground next to the trainer. The dog realizes that this is a reward for returning. Soon the dog learns not to roam far from its handler.

During a hunt, the dog might need to be given directions to the fallen bird after it is shot. For this reason, Cacchio teaches the 1 ½- to 2-year-old dog to respond to directional commands. For this training exercise, dog and trainer head to a baseball diamond. Cacchio puts the dog on the pitcher's mound while he stands on home plate. Cacchio has placed dummies, oblong pieces of canvas or plastic, on the three bases. The goal is to have the dog retrieve the

A retriever is a soft-mouthed dog that can carry a bird back to a hunter without tearing it apart.

dummies from the base on the dog's right or left side. To accomplish this training task, Cacchio commands "over" as he extends either his right or left arm. If he wants the young dog to work farther away from him, the trainer will give the command "back."

Hunters want a dog that is soft-mouthed, which means the dog can carry a bird without tearing it to bits. Some hunters may use a method called "forced retrieve" to train their dogs. With this method, hunters put a bird in the dog's mouth and pinch the dog's ear or toe to force it to hold the prey. Cacchio, however, doesn't use this kind of training.

"If the trainer has been too hard on the dog, the dog is hard on the bird," Cacchio explained. Instead, he uses a reward system to encourage the dog to hold the prey gently. This allows the dog to be treated kindly as it fulfills its retrieving purpose.

Cacchio has taught a number of dogs to hunt. The dogs and the hunters can spend an autumn day in the field, where the hunter can take pride in the performance of his hunting dog and its good flushing and retrieving abilities.

A Skillful Hunting Team

Master falconer Brian Bradley holds Prince, a Harris' hawk, on his left arm. He releases the strong raptor, and it spreads its huge wings and glides between the trees. Meanwhile, Bradley's miniature longhaired dachshunds race along the forest floor, swishing through leaves and brush. The dogs give yips of excitement as they catch the scent of a rabbit. The hawk perches on a high tree branch to watch the dogs' activities. The dachshunds flush the rabbit from beneath a log. The hawk darts from his branch

Brian Bradley, his dachshunds, and his Harris' hawk Prince work together during a hunt to carefully catch game.

perch, zooms in on the target, and kills the rabbit. The hunting team—humans and animals alike—will share a rabbit meal tonight.

Hunting with **raptors**, or birds of prey, has a long history. People began using raptors to help put food on the family table more than 4,000 years ago. Today, some falconers like Bradley, who train raptors, keep this hunting technique alive.

People that use raptors to hunt use the special ability of these birds to work as a team with their hunting dogs. Raptors are predators that devour other animals to survive. The word *raptor* comes from the Latin word *rapere*, which means "to seize or carry away." Raptors seize their prey with their strong feet and talons. Their hooked beaks help, too. Plus, their sharp eyesight, which is 8 to 10 times keener than human eyesight, is an excellent addition to any dog and human hunting team.

Raptors' bodies are specially designed for the environment in which they hunt. The accipiters, forest hawks, hunt from woodland perches. They have shorter, more rounded wings for maneuvering through the trees. Buteos are soaring hawks that hunt by gliding in the air, so they are equipped with long, broad wings. Bradley's Prince is a parabuteo and can hunt from perches or by soaring. He has long, broad wings.

Falcons soar thousands of feet in the open air and snatch their bird prey in mid-flight. They have long, narrow wings that are pointed at the tips, so they can fly at high speeds. Falcons that are diving straight down can reach speeds of more than 200 miles per hour (321.9 km/hr). These raptors also have long toes and a large foot spread, which help them catch fast prey the way a baseball player's mitt helps him catch a ball. Plus, a falcon has a notched beak that it inserts into the spinal cord of its prey to make the kill.

Bradley trained for years to become a master falconer. He had to pass a New York state test that evaluates a person's knowledge of the biology and training of raptors. The falconer-in-training then served a two-year apprenticeship under another falconer. If a person wants to earn the more advanced title of master falconer, like Bradley, he must have seven years of falconry experience and written recommendations from three master falconers.

Early in his falconer career, Bradley attempted to hunt with a hawk without using hunting dogs. He tried to flush small game by himself, but came home bloodied from run-ins with twigs and sticker bushes. Once, he almost lost an eye. That's when he realized there must be a better way.

The master falconer knew that hunters often used dogs in tandem with raptors to hunt more efficiently.

DOGS HELPING DEER

Picture this: A hunter in New York state shoots a deer, but the bullet only injures the animal. The mortally wounded deer runs into the forest. After hours of searching for the suffering deer, the hunter can't locate the animal. With a phone call to the Deer Search Inc. hotline, the hunter has a better chance of finding the deer in order to keep it from suffering further.

Deer Search sends one of its volunteer handlers and a blood-tracking dog, often a wirehaired dachshund, to the hunter's location. The handler attaches the dog to a 30-foot (9.1 m) lead, and the hunter, handler, and dog start to track the wounded deer.

The canine gathers the scent of blood from the spot where the deer was wounded. He puts his nose to the ground and tracks, following the scent of blood through sticker bushes and cold-water streams. Miles later, the dog finds the injured deer collapsed in a ditch. The hunter kills the deer with his shotgun, and the dog is rewarded with a bit of the meat and deer hide for its excellent tracking work.

(continues)

Deer Search uses wirehaired dachshunds, who have an excellent sense of smell, to track wounded deer.

(continued)

Donald Hickman and John Jeanneney established Deer Search Inc. in 1978 because they didn't want injured big game, such as deer or bears, to be in pain. The men knew that their wirehaired dachshunds could be trained to track the blood of wounded animals. The duo's dream was to volunteer their dog services to anyone who needed them.

Today, Deer Search helps hunters locate injured game. A variety of breeds, such as Labrador retrievers, mountain curs, and German shepherds, have joined the dachshunds in the search for injured animals. If the dog has a keen nose and can successfully follow a blood track, it is welcomed to help Deer Search care for animals in the wild.

He researched the different dog breeds he might partner with Prince, and he decided to purchase miniature longhaired dachshunds.

HOT DOGS FOR COOL WEATHER

Dachshunds are hounds that were originally bred in Germany for badger hunting more than 300 years ago. Because they are hounds, dachshunds have a well-developed sense of smell that they use to locate game.

Dachshunds are versatile dogs because, although they are hounds, they also chase prey right into their underground homes. With their extra-long bodies and short legs, dachshunds are just the right size and shape for entering the hole homes of small animals, such as badgers or rabbits.

Dachshunds have one of three coat types. Some of the dogs are smooth with short coats; others are long-haired, with lengthier fur. There are also wirehaired dachshunds that sport rough coats. Bradley considered the chilly weather of New York and decided on longhaired dachshunds so that the long fur would

Dachshunds come in different coat types, such as smooth-haired, longhaired, and wirehaired.

REPAIRING RAPTORS

Brian Bradley, his dachshunds Chase and Turq, his Harris' hawk Prince, and his **gyrfalcon** Dynamite spend their weekends at the Hudson Valley Raptor Center in Milan, New York. They educate adults and children about raptors and the injured birds that the center rescues. The Raptor Center takes in injured raptors that have suffered various injuries, such as gunshot wounds or broken wings. The center is able to heal more than half of the birds they rescue and return them to the wild.

The raptors that cannot be released stay at the center and make it their permanent home. People visit these raptors, as well as other birds of prey, including American bald eagles, snowy owls, and vultures.

During Bradley's program, Dynamite demonstrates high-speed dives and catches a bird decoy in midair. The dachshunds and hawk demonstrate how they work as a team. Audience members get a close-up look at the animals' capabilities.

Bradley explains to the audience that raptors play an important role in the environment. They help to control mammal and bird populations by taking the animals as their prey. Vultures keep the earth clean by feeding on dead **carcasses**. Vultures can also eat sick animals, like those with Lyme disease or rabies, without becoming ill themselves. In this way, these birds stop sicknesses from spreading.

Bradley stresses the need to keep birds of prey from being harmed. One way people can help keep raptors safe is by not littering. Often, night-hunting owls pick at scraps thrown along the side of a street. Drivers can't see the birds in the dark and accidentally hit them. By being mindful, everyone can play a part in keeping raptors safe.

keep the dogs warmer during hunting. He chose miniature dachshunds, which weigh less than 11 pounds (5 kg), because he needed small dogs that could easily enter tiny holes in the ground or squeeze through tight spaces in rock walls. Once Bradley decided to use dachshunds, the journey began to train his falconry canines to have a rewarding hunt.

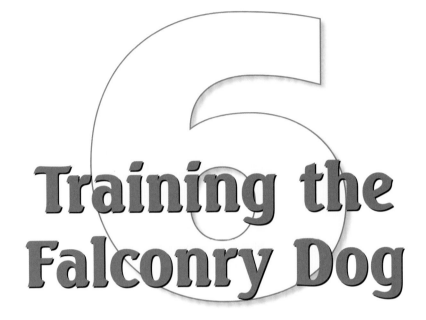

Training the Falconry Dog

Brian Bradley knew that the first step to raising a worthy falconry dog was to choose a promising pup. First, he researched and located respected breeders of working miniature dachshunds. After connecting with a breeder, he looked for certain personality characteristics when picking a puppy from the litter. He wanted a pup that was assertive and outgoing. The dog would have to forcefully track down game and be tough when it faced testy or hostile prey. In addition, he wanted a puppy that would put its nose to the ground and curiously explore the world, a necessary trait for tracking quarry. He also looked for a pup that would follow its littermates because dachshunds learn to hunt by watching older, more experienced dogs.

After much consideration, Bradley purchased his now 4-year-old female, Chase, and his now 1-year-old

HANDLING A HOT DOG

Dachshunds were originally bred for hunting badgers. In fact, the breed's name means "badger dog" in German. Dachshunds are hounds that hunt using their keen sense of smell.

A dachshund's extra long body and short legs make it the perfect shape for entering a badger hole. Unfortunately, its hot dog shape also leaves the dog in danger of developing back problems, known as canine intervertebral disk disease. This disease affects the disks, which act as cushions between the bones of the spinal column. Disk disease can cause the dachshund great pain or even paralyze it.

Dachshund owners can help their dogs avoid spinal injuries by reducing any unnecessary stress on the dog's spine. Owners shouldn't overfeed their dogs because extra weight causes added stress on the disks. Dachshund owners should also monitor the dog's activity, as it should not jump from furniture or climb stairs frequently.

Care should be taken when lifting or holding a dachshund because of the dog's delicate spine and rib cage. The dog's entire length of the body needs to be supported and kept horizontal to the ground. Holding this breed in a "football" hug—the way you would hold a football—is the best way to make sure the dog stays healthy and happy.

male, Turq. Bradley had to train each of these pups to hunt together with their hunting mate hawk, Prince.

When each of his pups was eight weeks old, Bradley taught each key obedience commands. The pups learned "come," "sit," and "no." He needed the dogs to respond to these commands to keep them safe while hunting in the woods.

To get the puppies and the hawk accustomed to one another, Bradley allowed the animals to spend time together while the hawk was tethered to a perch. He taught the dogs not to bother the bird, and the hawk learned that the dogs were not his next meal.

How did the falconer train the wild raptor not to attack the dogs? He placed the dogs near the hawk before the bird's feeding time. The raptor was rewarded with food for respecting the pups. On the other hand, if the bird behaved aggressively toward the puppies, Bradley did not reward the hawk with food. The raptor quickly learned to play nicely with the dogs.

After their basic obedience training and socializing, the dogs had their first hunting experience. He took the dachshunds into the woods and let them sharpen their natural hunting abilities. Both the excitement of the hunt and the meat of the prey, which the dogs shared with the hawk, became immediate rewards for the puppies.

During the hunt, the dogs got additional training. Because New York regulations do not allow dogs to hunt deer, Bradley had to teach the dachshunds not to track the scent of deer. If his dogs chased deer, he would stop the hunt and go home. The dogs quickly learned that if they wanted the thrill of the hunt, deer were off limits.

THE RIGHT DOG FOR THE JOB

Chase, Turq and Prince make a wonderful hunting team. However, Bradley can't pair the dachshunds with his gyrfalcon, Dynamite. Dachshunds flush the game as soon as they locate it. Falcons like Dynamite make wide circles thousands of feet high in the sky. For this reason, Dynamite needs to partner with a dog that indicates a game bird and waits for the perfect moment to flush it.

Pointers are good choices for a well-timed flush that coordinates with a gyrfalcon's flying pattern. These dogs detect a game bird's scent in the air and follow it. When the pointers are close to the prey, they point and remain still. The falconer watches to be sure that the bird is in position to make a successful strike, and he gives the dog the command to flush.

Falconers who hunt waterfowl might use retrievers for successful hunts. Retrievers flush water birds, such as ducks, into the air. Ducks are terrified of falcons, but a retriever's flush is aggressive enough to

Birds of prey are excellent animals to pair up with hunting dogs, as long as the dog's skills match the bird's instincts.

start the waterfowl flying. Then, the falcon swoops in, snatches the bird in midair, and brings it to the hunter. The tag team creates an exciting hunting experience for the human and the trained animals.

Gathering for the Border Collie

The handler and his black-and-white border collie enter the field. A flock of sheep stands grazing in the pasture. The handler holds a shepherd's crook, a long staff with a curve at the top, in his hand. He has a whistle tied around his neck. The handler whistles a command: "Away to me." The dog responds by running counterclockwise around the sheep. What happens next is a telltale sign that border collies are born to herd.

When the dog is behind the sheep, the handler tells it to lie down. The border collie stops in a crouch, with its shoulders down and its rear end up. The dog glares at the sheep. This stare is called "eye," and it helps convince the sheep to move away from the dog. "Walk up" the handler orders, and the dog slowly approaches the sheep. The sheep gather, as if following the dog's strict orders. The border collie collects the herd and walks the sheep directly to the handler.

The border collie has a natural instinct to gather stock and bring it toward the handler. With training

Border collies are known for their sharp intelligence. They understand almost 20 different herding commands.

These two border collies work together to gather the flock of sheep toward the farmer.

that builds on this natural ability, the border collie can be an invaluable tool to sheep farmers.

Border collies are superb herding dogs that are known for their intelligence. By the time they are trained to herd, border collies understand nearly 20 different commands. Border collies also have the ability to work independently. On big farms, the dogs often herd out of sight of their handlers and must solve problems on their own.

This dog breed has lots of energy and loves to herd. The dog's shoulder-down stance and staring "eye" make it seem like predators to the sheep. When a dog approaches the sheep herd like this, the group instinctively moves away. This is another reason border collies are successful at herding work.

TRAINING THE PUPS

Warren and Maria Mick own 11 border collies, and the dogs have won many championships at sheep herding trials. For the Micks and their pups, training begins when a dog is between 4 and 6 months of age as Warren teaches the dogs some obedience and good manners. Using treats, he will train a dog to come as its name is called and to lie down on command.

DOGS HERDING GEESE

Coal, an 8-year-old border collie with an intense stare, does not herd sheep. His favorite chase is geese. That's because Coal works for Geese Police based in Howell, New Jersey. Why does Coal herd geese?

"Canada geese produce between 1 and 1 ½ lbs. of droppings a day," says Joe Kohl, Geese Police's sales manager and Coal's handler. In addition, these messy geese can be aggressive toward people. Coal's job is to herd the birds until they leave an area.

Canada geese take up residence in places that have large sections of cut grass and bodies of water. This includes golf courses, airports, and public parks. Geese that live on airport property can collide with airplanes during takeoffs or landings. The crashes sometimes injure or kill plane passengers. Geese Police and other firms help rid these places of the annoyance of geese.

The most important part of this early training is to establish a good working relationship with the handler. The dog must learn to listen carefully to what its master says.

Typically, Mick introduces his border collies to sheep when they are between 8 and 10 months old. Pups any younger than this are too small and might become injured by the sheep. He begins with 5 to 10 sheep that are accustomed to being worked by dogs and that have easygoing personalities.

At first, the trainer lets the pup develop his instinct for herding while practicing in a small field. He lets the dog become used to coming behind the sheep

Geese Police purchase their border collies from top breeders. At 12 to 15 months old, the dog learns to herd sheep. Gradually, it advances to herding Indian runner ducks, which are simpler to herd than Canada geese because they can't fly and tend to stay in a group. Then, the dog learns to herd domestic geese and, finally, Canada geese. The training can take up to four years.

Geese Police looks for border collies that won't bite the geese. Hurting geese is inhumane and illegal. The Migratory Bird Act Treaty of 1918 makes it against the law to kill certain birds that migrate, including Canada geese. "Properly used, properly trained border collies are the most effective nonlethal control of Canada geese," Kohl explains.

People watch in amazement as Coal works. The dog is well trained and quickly follows commands. "It's like having a remote control on the dog," says Kohl.

and bringing them to him. Sheep normally go in the direction their heads are turned, and the dog learns to expect this. At this point, Mick does not use verbal commands.

Next, Mick introduces balance exercises. Border collies will naturally stay directly opposite the handler in order to keep the sheep from escaping. So he stands on one side of the sheep with the dog on the other side of the herd.

Imagine that the trainer and the dog are the opposite ends of a wheel's spoke. Mick moves to his right and the dog walks counterclockwise to keep this balance. Mick commands "away to me," so the dog associates his counterclockwise movement with this order. When Mick moves to his left, he tells the dog, "come bye." This readies the dog for a clockwise movement.

The border collie must learn to stay a certain distance from the herd. The dog has to be close enough to motivate the sheep, but not so close that the sheep become spooked and run. The handler uses the "walk up" command to place the dog at the proper distance, about 5 to 10 yards from the sheep. "Walk up" tells the dog to walk slowly in a straight line toward the sheep.

In more advanced training, a border collie learns to move, or drive, the sheep herd away from the handler. Driving is difficult to teach a border collie because it goes against the breed's gathering instinct, to move the sheep toward the farmer. Driving is easier for the dog to learn if the sheep are placed in a narrow lane with fences on either side and with the handler and the dog behind the herd. This way, the dog cannot race around the sheep and gather them back to the handler. Soon, the dog will grasp the driving concept and the enclosed area will no longer be needed.

Sometimes a farmer needs to bring only part of the herd into the barn or one sheep in for a veterinary check. Border collies can learn to separate one or

A border collie uses a shoulder-down stance and intense stare to move a group of sheep.

more sheep from the herd, a skill called **shedding**. Shedding is tricky for a border collie, whose instinct tells it to keep the herd together. At first, the handler will separate the sheep and call the dog to hold the ones that have been shed. Eventually, the dog will learn to separate the sheep by coming toward the sheep quickly and causing them to split.

Once the border collie responds consistently to verbal commands, Mick introduces whistle commands. The whistles can be delivered with multiple tones and speeds, as if the handler is conversing with the dog.

Like Australian cattle dogs, border collies can also herd larger animals, such as cattle and bulls.

For example, Mick might give a slow "come bye" whistle if he wants the dog to travel in a wide circle around the sheep. With practice, the dog learns to respond to the subtle commands of the whistle.

When the training is complete, the border collie and handler can spend productive days working the sheep. This energetic, intelligent dog will save the handler much effort as the human and canine team moves the sheep around the farm.

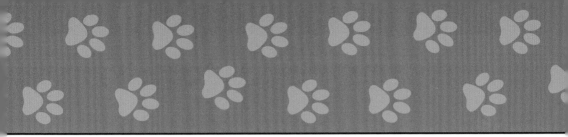

Driving the Herd

Imagine a spunky dog that has the courage to nip at the heels of a bull to encourage it to move. This canine is an Australian cattle dog, a brave and intelligent animal that is able to drive an entire herd of cattle to a new grazing spot. The breed originated in Australia, where dogs were needed to move wild cattle through the rough terrain of the Outback.

Australian cattle dogs are driving herders. The dogs have a natural instinct to drive cattle from behind, and to push the herd away from the handler.

Australian cattle dogs are spunky herding dogs that originated in the outback of Australia, where they were used to move wild cattle.

These dogs do not crouch down low, like the border collie, to convince the stock to walk. Instead, the Australian cattle dog stands upright on his four legs to herd. This breed doesn't even use a strong stare to make the cow move.

Australian cattle dogs must be fearless and strong to be able to move such large animals. The dog might boldly bite at the cattle's legs and then flatten itself to the ground to avoid a defiant kick from an unhappy steer. If a hoof hits the dog, it must recover quickly and continue herding. At times, an Australian cattle dog may find itself head-to-head with a stubborn 1,500-pound (680.4 kg) bull that must be herded. The spitfire canine may bite the bull smack on the nose to convince it to get moving.

WORKING WITH AUSTRALIAN CATTLE DOGS

When Cindy Vandawalker isn't busy training service dogs for Canine Working Companions in Waterville, New York, she trains her Australian cattle dogs to compete in herding trials, which are contests that test and rank the ability of herding dogs.

When Vandawalker chooses an Australian cattle dog from a litter of pups, she looks for certain qualities that may indicate a good driving dog. She pops open an umbrella near the pup. Vandawalker wants to see a puppy that will investigate the umbrella after the initial surprise of the noise. This demonstrates confidence, and an Australian cattle dog needs to possess confidence to challenge enormous animals each day.

The trainer looks for a puppy that will follow her around the yard. Australian cattle dogs need to feel comfortable around people so they can go through serious training and daily work with a handler.

Even though the herding styles of the border collie and Australian cattle dog are different, their training is similar. Vandawalker starts training the young dog

Australian cattle dog puppies need to feel comfortable around people before they can begin to train for herding.

to herd using sheep because they are smaller than cattle and less dangerous to the novice dog. She and the dog practice balance exercises, where he learns the directional commands "away to me" and "come bye." The dog is also taught to respond to the order "walk up." In time, it learns to act when whistle

THE HERDING BREEDS

Historically, herding dogs have been bred to do the particular job the herdsman required of them. In Britain, herding dogs were needed to gather flocks of sheep from large farms and bring them in for shearing. British herding dogs include the border collie, bearded collie, old English sheepdog, rough-coated collie, smooth-coated collie, and the Shetland sheepdog.

Herding dogs of continental Europe, known as continental herding dogs, kept watch over sheep on smaller farms. These dogs were used to keep the herd from trampling or munching crops, which were often found next to the grazing pastures. Continental herding dogs also had to protect the sheep from predators, so their assertive, protective nature was a big help. German shepherd dogs, briards, Bouvier des Flandres, Belgian Malinois, and Belgian sheepdogs are protective herding dogs.

Another group of canines worked with herds but did not round up the animals. These dogs were strictly bred to protect the herd from predators, both animal and human. Large, powerful canines, such as the Great Pyrenees and the komondor, kept protective watch over herds of sheep or cattle. Interestingly, the komondor's coat is made up of long white cords that allowed it to blend in with a herd of sheep. That way, the dog could go unnoticed in the herd until it was time for the canine to ward off the predator.

commands are issued. Once the young dog completes initial training, it advances to herding cattle.

Over the years of working with these canines, Vandawalker has observed the amazing spirit of the Australian cattle dog. One day, the trainer's 6-year-old male Australian cattle dog, Rocky, was herding goats. One of the goats butted the dog and sent him flying. Rocky shook off the pain and went right back to herding that stubborn goat.

Vandawalker has also had some funny experiences with her trained dogs. One warm afternoon, she watched in amazement as Rocky herded her young grandchildren away from a wading pool. Rocky must have decided that water, no matter how shallow, was a danger zone for small children.

When a cattle rancher wants a good herding dog, the Australian cattle dog is a fine choice. A dog of this breed will help round up the cattle and drive the herd anywhere the handler desires. This well-trained breed helps make a cow rancher's work much easier.

From obeying commands to following scents to herding sheep (or geese!), hunting and herding dogs provide great help to their owners. Without these dogs' unique abilities, people would have a difficult time hunting and herding successfully.

Glossary

Burrows holes in the ground made by animals (such as rabbits or foxes) for shelter or protection

Carcasses the dead body of an animal that's usually used as meat

Flush chase from a hiding place

Game animals hunted for food, sport, or hobby

Game birds birds, such as pheasants or quail, hunted for food, sport, or hobby

Gyrfalcon a large bird of prey that breeds on the Arctic coast and islands of North America, Europe, and Asia

Huntsman during a foxhunt, a person who directs and controls the foxhounds

Quarry an animal or bird hunted as game or prey

Raptors birds of prey that have a hooked beak and sharp talons to grasp prey

Shedding separating one or more sheep from a flock during herding

Track follow a specific scent in order to find something or someone

Whipper-in the person at a foxhunt who is responsible for the care and safety of the hounds

Bibliography

"About Foxhunting." Masters of Foxhounds Association of North America. http://www.mfha.com/abfo.htm

Adamson, Eve. "Oh My Aching Back." *Dachshunds*. Vol 10. pp. 76–83.

Allen, Mary. "The Dachshunds of Deer Search." Reprinted from *Dog World*. November 1995. 32–33. http://www.deersearch.org/dogworld.htm

Bailey, Joan. *How to Help Gun Dogs Train Themselves.* Hillsboro, Ore.: Swan Valley Press, 1992.

Beauchamp, Richard G. *Australian Cattle Dogs: A Complete Pet Owner's Manual.* Hauppauge, N.Y.: Barron's, 1997.

Beaufort, Hugh Arthur FitzRoy Somerset. *Fox Hunting.* Newton Abbot, Devon: David and Charles Publisher Ltd., 1980.

Beebe, Frank Lynn, Harold Melvin Webster, and James H. Endersen. *North American Falconry and Hunting Hawks.* Denver, Colo.: North American Falconry and Hunting Hawks, 1964, reprint 1989.

Bradley, Brian (Sky Hunters, Falconer and Dachshund Handler). Interview with the author. Hudson Valley Raptor Center, Milan, N.Y. June 19, 2005.

Cacchio, Raymond "Jerry." (Nationally renowned Hunting Dog Trainer and Handler). Interview with the author. Clinton, N.Y. December 5, 2005.

Canaday, Pat. (Border Collie Handler). Interview with the author. Rhinebeck, N.Y. October 15, 2005.

Cannavino, Suzie York (Rombout Hunt Club, Master of the Foxhunt). Telephone interview with the author. April 7, 2005.

Carroll, Terence. *Diary of a Fox-hunting Man.* London: Hamish Hamilton Ltd., 1984.

Corbin, Priscilla. "To Fly Again." *Dutchess Magazine.* July/August 2005. pp. 22–30.

Cowan, Nancy. "From the Earth to the Sky." *Dachshunds.* Vol. 10. pp. 65–69.

Derr, Mark. *Dog's Best Friend: Annals of the Dog-Human Relationship.* New York: Henry Holt and Company, 1997.

Derr, Mark. *A Dog's History of America.* New York: North Point Press, 2004.

Devine, Michael. *Border Collies: A Complete Pet Owner's Manual.* Hauppauge, N.Y.: Barron's, 1997.

Elman, Robert. ed. *Hunting Allies.* Broomall, Pa.: Mason Crest Publisher, 2002.

Falk, John R. *Gun Dogs.* Stillwater, Minn.: Voyageur Press, 1997.

Farren, Christopher. *Dogs on the Job: True Stories of Phenomenal Dogs.* New York: Avon Books, 2003.

Farrin, Stephen (Rombout Hunt Club, Professional Whipper-in). Interview with the author. Town of Clinton, N.Y. April 5, 2005.

Ford, Emma. *Falconry: Art and Practice.* London: Cassell and Company, 1992.

Garner, Ann. "Herding Style is Not A Fashion Statement." *Working Dogs Cyberzine.* 1997. http://www.workingdogs. com/doc0157.htm

Glasier, Phillip. *Falconry and Hawking.* Woodstock, N.Y.: The Overlook Press, 1998.

Gorrell, Gena K. *Working Like a Dog.* Toronto: Tundra Books, 2003.

"Herding Dogs and Livestock Guardians." Dogs with Jobs. http://www.dogswithjobs.com/about_dogs/training_tips/ training_pix/dog_jobs/herding_dogs.html

Hickman, Penny (Deer Search, Inc., Board Member and Dachshund Handler). Interview with the author. Pleasant Valley, New York. December 8, 2005.

"History of Deer Search Inc." Deer Search. http://www. deersearch.org/history.htm

Holland, Vergil S. *Herding Dogs Progressive Training.* New York: Howell Book House, 1994.

Howden, Laura. "Is the U.S. Safe from Foxhunting Debate?" *National Geographic News.* May 31, 2002. http://news. nationalgeographic.com/news/2002/05/0530_020532_fox. html

Hudson Valley Raptor Center. "Teacher Previsit Packet." 2004.

Imperati, Joy (Rombout Hunt Club, Field Master). Interview with the author. Town of Clinton, N.Y. April 5, 2005.

Kallen, Stuart A. *Collies.* Edina, Minn.: Abdo and Daughters, 1998.

Kohl, Joe. (Geese Police Inc. sales manager and border collie handler). Telephone interview with the author. July 21, 2006

Krause, Bob. (German Shorthaired Pointer Handler). Interview with the author. Cape May, New Jersey. July 2, 2005.

"MFHA Code of Hunting Practices." Masters of Foxhounds Association of North America. 2000. http://www.mfha. com/code.htm

Margolis, Matthew and Catherine Swan. *The Dog in Your Life*. New York: Random House, 1979.

Mick, Warren (North East Border Collie Association, Board Member, Border Collie Trainer and Handler). Interview with the author. Rhinebeck, N.Y. October 15, 2005.

Pickett, William. *Risk in the Afternoon: Some of the Pleasures and Perils of Foxchasing*. Middletown, Del.: Red Fox Publishing, 1998.

Rice, Philip F. and John I. Dahl. *Hunting Dogs*. New York: Harper and Row, 1967.

Slater, Kitty. *The Hunt Country of America*. New York: Aero Publishing, 1973.

Smith, Jason. *Dog Training: Retriever and Pointing Dogs*. Chanhassen, Minn: Creative Publishing International, 2003.

Vandawalker, Cindy (Canine Working Companions, Head Trainer and Australian Cattle Dog Handler). Telephone interview with the author. November 21, 2005.

Bibliography

Taylor, David. *The Ultimate Dog Book*. New York: Simon and Schuster, 1990.

Wilcox, Charlotte. *The Collie*. Mankato, Minn. Capstone High/Low Books, 1999.

Find out more about the training and work of the dogs in this book by contacting these organizations.

American Border Collie Association
82 Rogers Road
Perkinston, MS 39573-8843
601-928-7551
www.americanbordercollie.org

Deer Search Inc.
The Founding Chapter
P.O. Box 853
Pleasant Valley, NY 12569
www.deersearch.org

Hudson Valley Raptor Center
148 South Road
Stanfordville, NY 12581
845-758-OWLS
www.hvraptors.com

North American Hunting Retriever Association
P.O. Box 5159
Fredericksburg, VA 22403
540-899-7620
www.nahra.org

North East Border Collie Association
www.nebca.net/

Rombout Hunt Club
www.romboutfoxhounds.com/

United States Border Collie Handler's Association, Inc.
2915 Anderson Lane
Crawford, TX 76638
254-486-2500
www.usbcha.com/

Mesa County Libraries

Thank you for checking out the following items:

Renewed Items 11/14/2015 10:24
XXXXXXXXX7656

Item Title	Due Date
1090009146666	12/5/2015 00:00

1. Dog / written by Matthew Rayner ; photographed by Jane Burton.

1090007013517	12/5/2015 00:00

2. The true-or-false book of dogs / by Patricia Lauber ; illustrated by Rosalyn Schanzer.

1090009939453	12/5/2015 00:00

3. It's a dog's life : how man's best friend sees, hears, and smells the world / written by Susan E. Go

---

Checked out from the Central Library
www.mesacountylibraries.org
970-243-4442

Bass, Rick. *Colter: The True Story of the Best Dog I Ever Had*. Boston: Houghton Mifflin, 2001.

Beauchamp, Richard G. *Australian Cattle Dogs: A Complete Pet Owner's Manual*. Hauppauge, N.Y.: Barron's, 1997.

Collard, Sneed B. *Birds of Prey: A Look at Daytime Raptors*. New York: Scholastic Library Publishing, 2000.

DeLaurier, Art (ed). *Panther: And Other Stories of Great Hunting Retrievers: Original Stories about the Special Bonds Between Man and Dog*. Memphis, Tenn: Ducks Unlimited, 2003.

Elman, Robert. ed. *Hunting Allies*. Broomall, Pa.: Mason Crest Publisher, Inc., 2002.

Farren, Christopher. *Dogs on the Job: True Stories of Phenomenal Dogs*. New York: Avon Books, 2003.

Glaser, Rebecca Stromstad. *Border Collies*. Mankato, Minn: Pebble Books, 2006.

Graves, Russell A. *Hunting Dogs: A Photographic Tribute*. Iola, Wis: KP Books, 2002.

Gorrell, Gena K. *Working Like a Dog*. Toronto: Tundra Books, 2003.

Healy, Joseph. *Training a Young Pointer: How the Experts Developed My Bird Dog and Me*. Mechanicsburg, PA: Stackpole Books: 2005.

Norman, Geoffrey. *Riding with Jeb Stuart: Hunting Adventures with an English Pointer*. Guilford, Conn.: Lyons Press, 2005.

Trumbauer, Lisa. *Dachshunds.* Mankato, Minn.: Pebble Books, 2006.

Underwood, Lamar (ed). *The Greatest Hunting Stories Ever Told: Twenty-Nine Unforgettable Tales.* Guilford, Conn.: The Lyons Press, 2004.

VonRecum, Andreas F. *Hunting with Hounds in North America.* Gretna, La.: Pelican Publishing, 2002.

Web Sites

American Kennel Club
http://www.akc.org/breeds/index.cfm?nav_area=breeds
Investigate various dog breeds.

Dogs with Jobs
http://www.dogswithjobs.com/about_dogs/training_tips/
   training_pix/dog_jobs/herding_dogs.html
Read about all types of herding dogs.

Ducks Unlimited
www.greenwing.org
Learn about waterfowl and wetlands conservation through games and activities.

Masters of Foxhounds Association of North America
www.mfha.com/abfo.htm
Discover the history of the foxhunt and foxhunting today.

Picture Credits

Index